the basi

KITCHEN HACKS

AND HINTS

Best known in Britain as an entertaining and innovative TV chef, New Zealand born Glynn Christian began food broadcasts on London's LBC radio and BBC TV's Pebble Mill at One in 1982 and made over 1000 live broadcasts. He appeared three mornings weekly on BBC TV Breakfast Time and made the first TV food series shot abroad.

His UK journalistic career includes writing weekly for *The Sunday Telegraph* for four years for which he was nominated for Glenfiddich Food Writer of the Year, *Elle* magazine, where he was the original food editor, and work for *OK*, *House and Gardens*, *Gardens Illustrated*, as well as being the original cookery and food presenter on QVC Shopping Channel UK and then senior presenter on TVSN, Australia. He is the author of over 25 books mainly about food and cookery which include his best-known *REAL FLAVOURS—the Handbook of Gourmet and Deli Ingredients*, which was voted Best Food Guide in the World. Nigel Slater called it 'one of the only ten books you need'; Tom Parker Bowles says it is 'as important to the kitchen as a sharp knife'.

Glynn helped found The Guild of Food Writers and is the only food writer given a Lifetime Achievement Award from within the UK food industry, by the Guild of Fine Food, 2008 Great Taste Awards. He co-founded the iconic Mr Christian's Provisions on Portobello Rd.

He now lives in Battersea, London.

the basic basics
KITCHEN HACKS AND HINTS

350+ amazing tips for seasoned chefs and aspirational cooks

Glynn Christian

GRUB STREET • LONDON

Published in 2021 by
Grub Street
4 Rainham Close
London
SW11 6SS

Email: food@grubstreet.co.uk
Web: www.grubstreet.co.uk
Twitter: @grub_street
Facebook: Grub Street Publishing
Instagram: @grubstreet_books

A CIP catalogue record for this book is available from the British Library

ISBN 978-1-911667-10-0

The moral right of the author has been asserted

Printed and bound by Finidr, Czech Republic

CONTENTS

1

LIQUID ASSETS

MARTINI MAGIC

Freeze favourite olives and add to straight-up martini cocktails. They'll keep the drink ice cold without dilution. And then be delicious.

Choose a thick slice of frozen lemon if you prefer a twist.

Freeze pearl onions for a Gibson.

G&T PERFECTIONS

A goblet-shaped glass will enhance the G&T experience by trapping and enhancing aromas, whereas a straight-sided glass allows them to disperse

Preserve the coldness of the drink longer and avoid dilution of the gin by first chilling the glass with ice cubes and then pouring out any melted water.

Use only chilled gin and then chilled tonic water, because warm tonic will lose bubbles faster and the drink's vibrancy is reduced.

FRUIT ICE CUBES

To keep cocktails and soft drinks cold without diluting, freeze sliced lemon, lime or orange, cubes of melon, water melon, peach, whole cherries, grapes, raspberries, blue berries and more, and then use instead of ice cubes.

WATER ICE

Chill wine and champagne faster by using a mixture of ice cubes and water; it's quicker than just ice and will reach higher up the bottle.

FRUITY SUMMER WINE

Create happy faces and colourful tables with goblets of fruity red, rosé or white wine chilled by frozen berries or cubes of fruit. No dilution plus extra flavour and at least you might eat something.

NOT SO COSY

Use a tea cosy only when there are no tea bags or tea leaves in the pot. Tea brews, draws or mashes best in cooling water. A cosy keeps the temperature up and this extracts the bitter tannin content sooner than it should.

THE CUCUMBER GIN AND TONIC

Serve a single slice of cucumber in gin and tonic to transform it; once tried you'll never go back to lemon or lime.

TWO FOR TEA

Use a second, warmed teapot
if you don't take out the bags
or leaves once the tea is brewed.
Pour the perfect tea into that
and yes, this is when to use
a cosy. The second pot was
common right up until the 60s
and there were even newspaper
ads and infomercials in cinemas
to remind people. Then came
tea bags, the greatest advantage
of which is that they may be
removed when the brew is right.

COLD TEAS

Make a concentrated base for
crystal-clear iced tea by brewing
at least four tea bags overnight
in 300 mls/½ pint cold water;
using hot water makes it cloudy
as it cools. Drink as is over lots
of ice or dilute with sparkling
water, fruit juice, especially
pineapple, or with white wine
and sparkling water for a Tea
Spritzer. Sparkling white wine
is especially good with Rose
Pouchong or Earl Grey tea.

TEA OFF

Control your caffeine intake
from tea by heading East
through the day. Assam has the
most, followed by other Indians
except for fragrant Darjeelings,
and then it's Ceylon/Sri Lankan
or Kenyan. China Blacks have
less caffeine than those, followed
by Oolongs and then Green
tea to gentle you into the night.

SHARP WARNING

Use lemon to counteract
bitterness only in harsh, low-
grade teas. Used in higher grade
teas, lemon destroys the finesse
and fragrance you have paid for.

COFFEE GROUNDINGS

Pouring boiling water onto
ground or instant coffee destroys
the finest of the fragrant oils that
give the best flavour.

Pour less-than-boiling water
from a height onto instant coffee
or ground coffee; this cools it
on the way down and also aerates
the mixture.

Ignore advice that ground coffee should not be refrigerated. Tightly wrapped in its bag and stored in an airtight container, it will be fresh for weeks.

Freeze ground coffee tightly sealed and it is good for months, some say five months. Spoon out what you need and return to the freezer.

Using frozen coffee grounds means their temperature cools water that is too hot.

Get higher with Robusta coffee beans, which have a much higher caffeine content than Arabica beans, but a coarser flavour. Robusta beans are more likely to be used to make instant coffee, so this is commonly more stimulating than brewed coffee. Important to remember when following hacks to make super-caffeinated whipped coffees.

INSTANT WHIPPING I

Create Korean or Delgado whipped coffee with equal quantities of instant coffee, white sugar and water, which can be iced, ambient or hot: one or two tablespoons of each are a good starting point. Beat for three or more minutes to form a thick foam that peaks like meringue.

Serve over hot or cold milk, including nut milks.

Top cocoa or hot chocolate to make mocha heaven.

Pile onto brownies, chocolate or other cakes.

Finish ice-cream sundaes.

Heap onto sparkling water to make coffee soda like no other.

INSTANT WHIPPING II

Serve Greek frappé as a less caffeinated whipped coffee, a drink that's even found made to order in bars. In Corfu, three versions differ according to sweetness:

→ Straight (*sketos*) 1–2 teaspoons of instant coffee and no sugar.

→ Medium (*metrios*) 1–2 teaspoons of instant coffee with two teaspoons of sugar.

→ Sweet (*glykos*) 1–2 teaspoons of instant coffee with four teaspoons of sugar.

Combine your choice with 2–3 tablespoons of water and shake to create a stable foam. You can also use a milk frother or a milkshake maker. Pour over ice cubes in a tall glass, adding water, sparkling water or milk to taste— perhaps a mixture.

Fool frappé-heads into thinking you are part of the head-high gang by using de-caffeinated instant.

DOUBLE PLUNGING

Plunge a cafetière immediately after pouring on the water and then return to the top, which ensures the grounds are evenly wet and will brew fully. Then brew less time than you would usually do.

SKIMMING THE TOP

Froth only skimmed milk because it makes firmer frothed milk for hot coffee; it is protein not fat that makes the foam. Even made with a hand beater rather than in a dedicated foam-producer, skimmed milk will hold its shape better than full milk.

DROP SHOTS

Drop a square of high cocoa-solids chocolate (70%) into espresso for a maxi-mocha. Trending high cocoa-solids milk chocolates add creaminess.

2

EGGSACTLY

FLOATERS AND SINKERS

Check egg freshness in a bowl or jug of water. Fresh eggs lie on the bottom, those that stand tippy-toe are OK, any that float should be discarded.

SHELL BE RIGHT X 2

Boil eggs direct from the refrigerator without cracking their shells by starting in cold water. When the water boils, cook them your preferred time.

If your eggs are room temperature, they won't crack if you prick both ends of the shell with a needle before putting into gently boiling water.

NAILED IT

Wet your fingers if long acrylic nails make it tricky to pick up eggs or to take them from a carton.

QUELLING QUAIL EGGS

Keep quail eggs warm to peel easily. Cook and then almost cool in running water. Roll over a worktop to crack the shells and then put back into warm water so that seeps under the shells. It's letting the membranes get cold that makes shelling difficult.

HARD FACTS

You'll try harder to peel hard-boiled very fresh eggs.

Crack the shells of hard-boiled eggs while they are cooling under running water; do this easily by vigorously shaking the pan. This avoids a black ring forming around the yolk and usually makes shelling easier.

Use a pasta server to move slippery eggs after shelling.

NET RESULTS

Fry shelled hard-boiled eggs in olive oil and create a golden, webbed net around each.

Dip into spice mixtures, like cinnamon, cumin and salt, or coriander and salt, or garam masala and salt. Chopped parsley or fresh coriander, too.

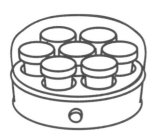

NIGHT EGGS

Simmer eggs in their shells at least eight hours, or overnight, and both whites and yolks develop melting tenderness. These are even better if fried as above once shelled.

Add onion skins to the water, which will lightly colour the eggs.

Spices or herbs in the water will scent the egg; you get a bigger flavour if these are regularly changed for fresh ones. Serve the same spices and herbs in any dip for the eggs.

SIMULTANEOUS SERVICE

Start and finish fried or poached eggs for a crowd at the same time: first break the eggs into a bowl and then tip them into the pan all at once.

PRE ORDER

Poach eggs in advance and remove from the water. When reheated in water or fried, they will not cook more but stay the same liquidity.

BEATING RETREAT

Eggs for meringues and soufflés should be at least two days old and four or five is better, as the whites of very fresh eggs do not give the best volume or texture.

3

BAKING STUFF

COOL HANDS

'Hot hands' make it impossible to rub butter into flour without it becoming a paste rather than crumbs, so:

→ Freeze the butter and grate it into the flour. By the time it is rubbed in, it will only just have thawed.

→ Rub the butter and flour together high over the bowl and let it drop back from that height; this keeps heat out of the bowl and the crumbs cool as they fall.

BETTER BUTTERING

Grate frozen butter onto anything about to be baked, rather than dabbing and dotting unevenly. Keeps hands clean, too.

EVEN PIECES

Mix only three-quarters of dried fruits or nuts into a cake mixture. Add the last quarter of the dry ingredients into the remaining batter when about two thirds through transferring to the baking tin, because that portion usually has fewer fruits mixed in.

DON'T DROP IT

Spoon cake batters into baking tins for a lighter result. Pouring cake mixes bounces out some of the air you have incorporated, especially from sponge mixtures.

SWEET SPOONING

Avoid honey and time waste by dipping a spoon quickly into oil and draining or running under hot water before spooning out honey, liquid or creamed.

NO MUFFIN SECONDS

Spoon muffin mixtures into tins or paper cases with a single blob. A second spoonful can make muffins heavy.

SCONESENSE

True scones never contain eggs.

Scone mixing should be done with a table knife and then never rolled but patted into shape.

Cut with sharpest blade possible, so edges are not smeared and scones can rise fully.

Round and fluted cutters must be sharp and deeper than the mixture is thick, so the edges are not smeared, which inhibits rising.

Ideally, preheat and flour the baking tray and shape the scones on that.

Transfer baked scones to a cooling rack and leave them alone to keep crustiness, cover with a clean cloth for soft scones.

Pull hot or cold scones apart rather than cutting, which smears and flattens the light texture.

FLAT OUT

Spread the top of fruit cake mixtures towards the sides before baking, leaving a depression in the centre, and you are more likely to get the admired flat surface.

FLAT IN

Screw baking parchment into a ball before lining a tray. When it's flattened it stays like that rather than curling.

MAKING MATCHES

Make a shallow cut from top to bottom before slicing a cake horizontally prior to adding a filling. Replace the layer or layers exactly by aligning the cut. Otherwise, insert a cocktail stick above and below where you slice across and realign those.

HOT RELEASES

Release a reluctant cake that has cooled too long in the tin, by holding it over gentle heat, which will melt butter or other fat on the base. Not a problem if you have lined with baking parchment.

COCOA FLOURING

Use cocoa powder instead of flour when preparing a baking tin for a chocolate cake. No white smudges on the cooked cake and the flavour will be heightened, too.

SHINY ICING

Aim a hair-dryer at a freshly iced cake, which will slightly melt and shine the surface. Practise on left-over icing because too much heat makes the icing melt and run.

FIRST SLICE EASE

Cut a neat first slice of any pie, tart, flan, quiche, whatever, that's baked and served from a dish with sides:

→ Fold a doubled piece of aluminium foil into a wedge shape slightly narrower than an ideal serving and put in before the pastry. The piece must be long enough to fold up the inside of the pan and over the lip. Bake the usual way.

→ To serve the first slice, cut just outside the edges of the foil wedge and then use the tab over the edge to lift it.

REALLY WHEELY

Use a pizza wheel rather than a knife for more control when cutting shallow tarts and flans.

ROLL OVER

Transport pastry to dishes by rolling it lightly around a pin and then unrolling directly above the baking tin or pan.

LUMPING TO LIKE IT

Use a small lump of pastry to push pie crusts firmly into the bottom of the tin and into any fluting, ensuring sharp edges and no puncturing.

BLIND LEADING

An easier way to use beans or other weights when blind-baking is to keep them in an ovenproof roasting or baking bag, much easier to distribute evenly over the pastry and to remove, and you can use the same roasting bag many times.

Otherwise, to ensure a pre-baked base is cooked through and that the edges stay upright, make a thick circle of crumpled cooking foil and arrange this close to the upright crust.

FIRMER BOTTOMS

Brush a still hot, blind-baked pastry case for anything savoury with lightly whisked egg white and let this set before adding the filling.

For something sweet, spread lightly melted chocolate onto a blind-baked pie crust, defending it from attacks from the filling and adding a surprise.

PIES TO GO

Choose short crust for the base and flaky or puff pastry for the top of any pies to be eaten in the hand because this gives a firmer crust that's easier to hold. Especially useful outdoors, whether for sweet or savoury, and *de rigueur* for a bacon and egg pie.

PROPER TARTS

Use a bulb baster rather than a spoon to fill individual tartlet cases, making it easier not to overfull or spill.

FREE-FORM ESCAPE

Avoid conventional fruit pies and present an open-topped galette instead. Roll pastry to a circle, top with sugared fruit leaving a wide edge and then turn the pastry to cover as much or as little as the filling as suits. Apple, peach, pear, pineapple and soft berries are the usual fillings.

QUICHE ME SLOW

Experience real Quiche Lorraine by filling only with a thin scatter of chopped green (unsmoked) bacon, perhaps with a little leek, and a custard of eggs and cream: one egg to every 150 ml. Blind baked pastry and then bake

slowly at less than 180°C/350°F. What happened to the British savoury tart? That was where spinach and salmon and cheese once went.

NO WHEY TO GO

Avoid baked egg-custard mixtures splitting into curds and whey by never cooking above 180°C/350°F. This is why these should be cooked in pre-baked cases, because the mixture cooks and sets before pastry cooks through but *see Portuguese Egg Tarts, page 22.*

SWEET TIMES—OR NOT

Judge cooking times for an egg-custard mixture by whether it is sweet or savoury.

The sweeter the mixture, the longer to set: a salty one sets faster.

FLOCCULATE ME

Move scrambled eggs very slowly with a broad spatula as they cook, so you encourage large soft clouds, a process known as flocculation.

PORTUGUESE TWISTS

Identify an authentic Portuguese Egg Tart (*pasteis de nata*) by checking for a swirl on the base of the pastry, made by doing the following, which creates the unique flower-like flaky upper edge:

→ Roll up puff pastry and slice into thin circles.

→ Lay each circle on an individual tart tin and push the pastry into the base by swirling with your thumb and thus forcing the edge to stand up exposed.

→ Fillings must be very sweet, so they do not split at the high temperatures needed to make the edges separate into frilly flowers.

PAVLOVA STEPS

Authentic Antipodean Pavlova has a thick, marshmallow centre and crisp crust, made by adding cornflour and vinegar to beaten egg whites and sugar. Without those two ingredients it's 'just a bloody meringue, mate!'
A topping of strawberries and passion fruit on whipped cream was the norm but now kiwi-fruit rules.

Control the otherwise free-form shape of a Pav by drawing around a plate on baking paper and piling within the circle.

CHEESECAKE CHEAT

For something faster and lighter than cheesecake, mix two parts of whipped cream with one part of crème fraîche or plain or flavoured thick yoghurt. Leave it alone for an hour or so and their acid thickens the cream.

CRÈME BRÛLÉE CHEAT

Make the above, put into ramekins (over raspberries?) and strew with muscovado or stronger-tasting molasses sugar, which will liquefy when you refrigerate it for an hour or more. No crust to crack but a rum-flavoured topping without a grill cracking your porcelain ramekins or blistering your skin.

CRUSTY THOUGHTS

Instead of digestive biscuits for a cheesecake crust, crush Italian amaretti for something original, sweet, chewy and very almondy.

Crumble dark chocolate digestives rather than plain ones and leave them slightly rough, so there are definite pieces of chocolate. Or add chopped chocolate.

And don't forget ginger biscuits, but include finely diced preserved or candied ginger.

SHINING IN
Use baking foil with the shiny side on the inside. If this is outside, it reflects heat and extends cooking time.

DONE FOR
Push a strand of uncooked spaghetti into a baking cake to check if it is done. If wet mixture is seen when it is withdrawn, it needs longer. A fine skewer or thin knife can also be used.

CRACKED IT
Repair a cracked cheesecake while still warm by surrounding it with a wide strip of doubled foil, doubled cling film, muslin or ribbon, pulling that tight

enough to close the crack and then securing firmly with a bulldog clip.

Or ignore it and cover with lightly crushed berries or a sweeter jam, especially cherry.

CRUMBLING SOLUTIONS
Get the crumble type you prefer, both better made by hand.

For crunchy crumble with buttery lumps, rub together equal weights of flour and butter, without making an even texture, and then stir in the same weight as the butter of sugar, white or demerara. Strew unevenly and without pressing down.

For a sandier crumble, use twice the weight of flour to butter, rub together to make an even texture and then stir in the same weight of white or demerara sugar as of butter. Spoon on rather than sprinkle and do not pat down.

DECONSTRUCTED CRUMBLE
Bake the first crumble mixture on a flat tray until brown, crisp and separate. Serve with separate bowls of cooked fruit

and of custard or cream and let everyone make the balance they like best. No more sludgy layers of undercooked crumble.

ROLLING ON

Roll flaky and puff pastries with short, sharp strokes. Long strokes can force air bubbles out of the layers.

PASTRY ROLLS

Forget pastry sticking to work surfaces:

→ Wrap cling film over a cutting board and secure it underneath. Dust lightly with flour.

→ Put baking paper or waxed paper over and under pastry and roll like that.

PASTRY PARTICULARS

Add flavour and interest to pastry as you roll, particularly to flaky and puff:

→ Sprinkle on sweet spices or grate orange, lemon or lime directly onto the pastry before you make the first turn.

→ Strew savoury spices, whole or ground, like fennel or cumin seeds, garam masala, baharat etc: good combined with orange zest. Add herbs, especially, rosemary, oregano and mint, dried or fresh.

A PROPER JOB

Thinly slice and layer rather than chop ingredients for a true Cornish pasty: beef, potato and swede; some like a little chopped onion but salt and plenty of pepper are musts. NO CARROT.

The number of crimps, top or on the side, is debatable, but should be at least 20.

WINE NOT

Instead of a rolling pin, use a full bottle of chilled white or rosé wine, which will keep the pastry firm; wrap it first in cling film to protect the label.

EXCESSIVE USE

When you have excess pastry hanging over a baking tin, cut off the untidy edges with kitchen scissors, because using a knife is liable to stretch the pastry.

Tuck excess pastry under the edge to make a double layer, which can then be pressed with a fork or crimped. Easier and more reliable than cutting off and adding a circle of leftover pastry to the rim.

UNDERCUT

Slice away excess pastry from a cooked blind-baked shell from inside to outside, or you will break away the crust and pieces will fall inside.

THE REST OF IT

Avoid pastry shrinking by planning your baking so the pastry can rest and chill before cooking, at least 30 minutes in a refrigerator.

ANGLE POISE

Slice choux buns and eclairs at an angle from the top down towards the opposite side, so the filling doesn't squeeze out when you bite; easier for decorating, too.

DECORATOR'S PLATES

Cobweb pastries, cake and pie slices:

→ Lightly flood a small plate with cream, thin custard or a fruit coulis; add a central blob of something contrasting and use a teaspoon to draw radiating lines from the centre to the outside. Serve the sweetness centrally on this.

→ Make a comma or apostrophe; place blobs of whipped or thick cream, custard, fruit coulis or thicker fruit or vegetable puree onto the serving plate. Point the tip of a teaspoon through the blob and then quickly draw out, curving as you do. Add extra drama by dripping a contrast into the centre and starting the teaspoon in that.

4

SAVING YOUR DOUGH

RAISING THE STAKES

Bread-dough and cake mixtures are raised by one of three different ways of creating bubbles within the mixture:

Baking powder: this is a mixture of chemicals invented in the mid-19th century. It works only in the presence of heat, as in an oven, and does not need gluten to work, so can be used with flours other than wheat.

Baking soda, also called bicarbonate of soda or sodium bicarbonate: do not confuse with washing soda, which is sodium carbonate. This is activated by mixing with an acidic liquid, like buttermilk or yoghurt. The action is immediate and means the dough must be mixed swiftly and put into the oven as soon as possible. Works best with wholemeal or white wheat flour.

Yeast is a live enzyme that ferments when mixed with flour and water, creating carbon-dioxide bubbles of elastic gluten that aerate or leaven wheat flour and some others. It cannot leaven a flour that does not contain gluten. Available in several forms:

→ As fresh or compressed fresh yeast.

→ As dried yeast granules, some types of which can be mixed directly into dough without being first activated.

→ As sourdough, which is a portion of previously made dough and known as a mother or starter.

→ As natural yeasts in the air, which will ferment a mixture of flour and water and then become a new starter giving different flavour characteristics according to the location it is made.

SODA, SO GOOD

Test baking powder for freshness by dropping a little hot water onto a teaspoon of it, or by stirring two teaspoonful into a cup of hot water. It should fizz. Cold water won't give a result.

WHEN YEAST GOES WEST

Sugar should only be used to activate dried yeast; it inhibits fresh yeast and should be mixed only into the flour mixture.

Salt also inhibits yeast and should not be incorporated into any activating mixture but mixed only into the flour blend.

BREAD QUICK SMART

Make soda bread in minutes, serve it within the hour. Although traditionally made with wholemeal flour, plain white flour makes a lighter loaf that is often more enjoyed.

Mix flours to make your own, including oat or barley flour.

You do not need to stretch gluten by kneading, instead mix lightly with a table-knife blade and knead only once or twice out of the bowl to even up the dough.

Put onto a preheated baking tray in a free-form circle then cut a deep cross two-thirds into the loaf and get it into the oven as quickly as possible, because baking soda works the moment it mixes with an acidic liquid.

White flour needs less soda than wholemeal and too much can add an unwelcome flavour. One teaspoon for 500 g white flour or a scant two for 500 g of wholemeal are good starting points to establish your preferences.

Soda bread does not, and should not, include baking powder or cream of tartar/tartaric acid; these make it a scone loaf.

SODA SO GOOD

Try plain yogurt as an alternative to traditional buttermilk in soda breads. Soured cream or crème fraîche give softer, sweeter loaves.

MEASURED THINKING

Remember the world uses two fluid measurements:

→ The UK and Australian pint is 20 fl oz/600 ml: half that is a cup measurement.

→ The USA, South Africa and New Zealand pint is 16 fl oz/500 ml: half that is their cup measurement.

SLICED BOTTOMS

Turn a very crusty loaf onto its side to cut, and your knife will more easily cut the tough bottom crust.

PULLING POWER

Never cut a hot or warm bread roll—and don't do it to cold ones either. This smears the inside and flattens it back to dough—and is an insult to the baker. Pull them apart, to protect the texture and make eating more pleasurable too. It's ok to insert a knife point to start off.

GARLIC BREAD

Slice a baguette lengthwise to make garlic bread, rather than into almost-slices. The butter is unlikely to leak so there is even less reason to wrap it in foil, which nastily steams and softens the bread. Let it cool to warm before slicing.

TWISTER SAVINGS

Keep bagels, buns and sliced bread fresh and neat by twisting the top of the wrapper tightly and then folding the excess back over and down around the remainders. Tidier and space-saving, too. Could also be used on other wrapped products.

CRUMBS

Slice off tough bottom crusts before making breadcrumbs and the result will be more even and better coloured.

NO-NEED

Forget kneading bread made with 100% wholemeal flour, as the wheat germ inhibits yeast action and you get a heavier loaf.

MONKEY AROUND

Amuse everyone by making Monkey or Pull-apart Bread next time you bake. Best done in a mould, add the dough in lumps, brushing the top of each with butter or olive oil and any other flavours that occur, sweet or savoury.

NOT STRAIGHT

Cut angles into baps for bacon or sausages, rolls for egg or any other salad, kaisers for ham or salami or any other filling. Slice at an angle from one side of the top towards the opposite base. Fillings and sauces don't squash out and they look much more generous.

SPACE OUT

Make even more space in angle-cut rolls by pulling out a little of the bread. Keep the crumbs in the freezer.

PIZZA SLICES

Use twice the usual yeast content to make bread dough as the base for genuine Neapolitan deep-dish pizza in a roasting pan or cake tins. Plenty of olive oil underneath and tinned tomatoes with all their own juices, lightly crushed. Then the usual suspects and much more olive oil.

Hide delicate buffalo milk mozzarella slices under the tomatoes but a better idea is only to add them after baking.

Strew on dried oregano for the elusive true taste of pizza.

EAST-WEST PIZZA-NAANS

Use hot, billowy naan bread instead of rice as a base for curries, dhals or meat stews and topped with fresh herbs and plenty of black pepper. Or do the same with a crisped pizza base.

Smear just-warm naan bread with crème fraîche or soured cream, top with smoked salmon and fresh basil leaves, perhaps also with a little black or white truffle oil, if you can forget the flavour is not real.

5

FISH AND NO BONES ABOUT IT

FRESH SIGNS

Ensure these when buying fresh fish:

→ The smell should be of salt or fresh water; nothing ammoniacal or strong.

→ Eyes should be bright and bulgy.

→ Gills must be bright red and not brown. Scales must be firmly attached.

FISH WAYS AND MEANS

Steam/poach fillets in one or two old-fashioned but forgotten ways:

→ Between two plates over boiling water. Butter, seasoning, perhaps some herbs but no liquid other than a splash of medium-dry white wine or white vermouth. The microwave does the same thing more simply and without steam in the kitchen.

INCHING

Bake fish gently using this broad guide: 10 minutes per 1 inch/2.5 cm thickness plus 10 minutes.

SKIN CONDITIONS

Skin a fish fillet from the tail end. Make a small incision through the flesh to the skin at the very end of the tail and then flatten the knife between the skin and the flesh. Grab the skin end behind the knife and then move the skin sideways to and fro while easing the knife forward. Blunter knives work better than sharper.

→ Poach fish in milk rather than water and use the milk to make a sauce: use water only as a last resort, even if it is highly flavoured, because so much fish flavour is left in the water. Heavily smoked or artificially coloured fish is best cooked in water, which should then be discarded.

→ Leave a whole salmon overnight in the poaching liquid to ensure moistness.

BOWLED OVER

Detect the pin bones in a side of salmon by first running the back of a knife over the flesh from tail to head end.

Then lay the salmon side skin-side down over a bowl and the arching will make the bones more obvious. Use tweezers.

SMALL BONES

Debone sardines and other small fish before cooking. Once gutted and cleaned, spread the fish belly down and press firmly from head to tail along the spine. Turn the fish over, and the skeleton should come out in one piece but double-check for left overs.

SALMON CATCH

Mix a tin of salmon with crushed salt crackers (Ritz, Saltines etc.), season with grated lemon zest, chopped parsley, a press of garlic and a little mayo. Leave 30 minutes for the biscuits to soften, shape into a patty and fry to heat through.

SMOKED SALMON PIE

Layer well-flavoured smoked salmon between thin pancakes, smeared with soured cream flavoured with a breath of horseradish, lemon zest, parsley and black pepper—at least four layers topped with a fifth. If it's for adults, sprinkle gin lightly, too. Leave several hours, expecting most filling to sink into the pancakes and hold everything together. Cut into wedges as perfect hand-held picnic fare but just as good with salad as a first course or light main. Slight sweetness in the pancakes is a good thing.

BELLY-STUFFED FISH

Gut fish by slicing along the spine rather than opening the

belly. Snip the spine behind the head and at the tail, carefully cut around both sides of the rib cage, remove this and then the guts and gills.

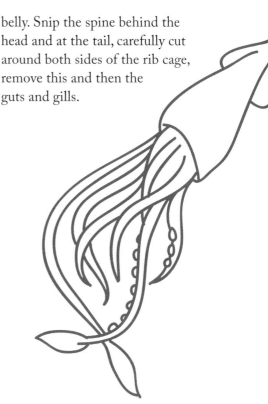

Season and stuff the interior, knowing it will not spill out during cooking and you can serve astonishingly whole fish without bones, serving in neat slices that include both sides and the stuffing.

KIPPER TIES

Eliminate (most) kipper smells by traditional jugging, putting them head down in a tall jug and filling that with boiling water. After five minutes, pour away the water and then slide out the kippers. Use a deep covered saucepan if you don't have a suitable jug.

RACKING UP

Barbecue fish between cake racks tied loosely together. Use tongs to turn them over.

SAUCE SOURCES

A little sweetness enhances white fish tastes, so add lemon *and* butter, or lemon *and* cream and wine, rather than just lemon juice.

Thus, use a medium-dry white wine to make sauces for fish, never a dry one; that is what you should drink too.

Finish cream sauces for fish with a few drops of sweet wine—even rich ports or a PX sherry, unless you use too much.

ROLL CALL

Roll flat fish fillets, especially sole, with the flesh side outwards

because there is a ligament that pulls the flesh into a curve when cooked; if done incorrectly the fillet will unfurl messily.

LESS LEMON

Zest lemon directly over smoked salmon rather than flooding with juice, to give a fresher flavour and better appearance; you will actually taste the salmon.

BEGONE!

Hiding the smell and flavour of stale or less-than-fresh oysters or caviar was why raw onion, shallots, spring onions and their mates were once served with them, especially after WWI. Or to make flaunting public consumption of them possible for people who simply didn't like them. The smell of raw onion was part of the plan to mask the palate, egg dulled the palate.

With today's better transport and refrigeration we should taste these rare treats naked:

→ Serve oysters unaccompanied, perhaps with a little lemon juice or grated lemon zest—no, absolutely no—onion, shallots, vinegar or chilli sauce.

→ Chew oysters at least once— otherwise what is the point of spending that money?

→ Be especially respectful of the finer flavour spectrum of the rare, flatter-shelled native oyster.

→ Cook or heat only coarser flavoured rock-oysters.

→ Touch caviar with no metal other than gold as they will interact to change its flavour: otherwise use bone, wood, semi-precious stones or plastic. Then, eat caviar by the unsullied spoonful or you'll never know what the fuss is about.

→ Accompany those spoonsfuls with unsalted butter on high-quality white bread or on warm unsweetened brioche.

MUSSEL MUSCLE

Double-check raw mussels are safe to eat, even when from a reliable source. Discard all that will not close before cooking and any that are broken. After cooking, don't serve or eat any that remain closed. Just to be sure.

6

BIRDS IN THE HAND

WISH AWAY

Remove the wishbone from roasting birds to make carving stress free. Before cooking, lift the neck skin and use a very sharp knife to cut around and then sever the wishbone. Leave it in place if you like but flick it away before carving. Especially good advice for Christmas turkeys and geese but for family chicken dinners, too.

GETTING ABREAST

Make carving and serving large turkeys faster and neater by removing each side of a cooked and rested turkey's breast meat in one piece:

Cut through the skin either side of the central breast bone and down to the carcass, then use a sharp pointed knife to cut the breast away from the bone and slice it off at the bottom. Cut into thick slices, which look great on the plate. Lots of gravy.

BUTTERFLY SAVING

Save at least 20% cooking time by butterflying your bird, small or large.

Cut either side of the backbone and remove.

Turn the bird over and spread the sides and then press down on the breast bone to break and flatten it.

Roast or grill, turning just once.

GETTING STUFFED

Stuff poultry under the skin or in the neck but NEVER in the cavity, as this can stop the inner bones cooking through and transfer food poisoning to the stuffing, which might be undercooked anyway. Stuffing or forcemeat was once only cooked under a spit-roasted bird or baked in balls around it.

DESTRUSSING

Remove all trussing from poultry before roasting and pull legs away from the body without breaking the skin.

Trussing was used to ensure spit-roasted birds turned evenly but means heat cannot get to the thickest part of oven-roasted birds, making it likely you overcook the breast while waiting for the legs to be done.

STOCK ANSWERS

Make richer stocks from poultry bones by first browning them. Roast or grill them carefully but deeply, or do this in a big saucepan, turning regularly. Cover with water and simmer at least two hours, with or without vegetables; add bay leaves and herbs only for the last 10–20 minutes. Strain and then use to cook rice by the absorption method or as a soup base.

Or reduce, cool and freeze in cubes as a handy addition to sauces, soups and gravies.

SAUCE SOURCES

Create super sauces for poultry by reducing cooking juices and then stirring in Boursin cheese, either the herb or the black pepper version.

DUCK IT

Ensure pan-fried or grilled duck breasts are tender by resting longer than you would a steak —at least 10 minutes. DON'T cover with cooking foil. Then slice at a very acute angle for the best look.

FRUITY RELATIONS

Serve more than orange sauces with duck and poultry:

→ Stir sliced fresh cherries into hot buttered rice and flavour lightly with ground allspice.

→ Do the same with sliced dates or micro-roasted almonds or walnuts, perhaps both. Torn parsley or coriander, too, of course.

→ Cook cranberries with orange zest and a little orange juice until they pop; add sugar only now or the skins will toughen.

→ Pan-fry thick slices of fresh pineapple in butter until the surfaces start to caramellise and then grind coarse black pepper onto both surfaces. Cook for a few minutes more so the pepper releases its full aromas. Perfection with duck.

→ Purée and strain raspberries, add roasting juices and then heighten with cider vinegar to make a sweet-sour flavour. Heat gently or the colour and flavour will dissipate. Very good with pheasant or grouse and a barley pilaff.

→ Flavour a sharp apple purée with a mix of orange and lemon zests, or with lime zest alone.

→ Purée canned red plums and cook on to thicken with a cinnamon stick, mace, several bay leaves and red wine. Finish with judicious additions of either brown sugar or citrus juice, maybe both.

→ Soak fresh, pitted dates in cream or PX sherry. Put into hot gravy at the last moment, or heat a little in the microwave and serve separately. Grate on lime zest for added intrigue.

MEATING
OF
MINDS

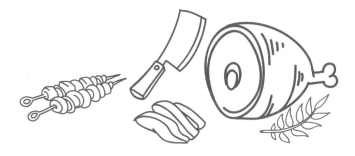

COLOUR STEAKS

Steak will not colour well if the surface is wet. Dry both sides with kitchen roll immediately before cooking, so it browns fully. This also applies if you have used a marinade.

OIL-FREE STEAK

Do not smear steaks with olive or other oil, as most kitchen extractors cannot cope with the resulting smoke; anyway the high heat denatures the oil and changes its flavour. A properly hot pan will give excellent colour to a steak with a dry surface.

JUDGE THE PERFECT STEAK

Bring steak to room temperature before cooking. Cook over high heat without flipping until you see the first drops of red liquid appear. Turn and cook until the same thing happens.

This gives medium-rare steak and you'll soon learn to judge how much juice appears before you choose to flip and serve, thus making the steak more or less done.

Do not press a steak with any instrument while it is cooking as this compacts and toughens the meat.

Do not use a splatter guard as it creates steam and toughens steaks. Instead, use a wire sieve as the height of the mesh above the food prevents the steaming caused by the closeness of a splatter mat.

Remove to a warm plate, season and then rest about ten minutes before serving, according to thickness.

Do not cover while resting as this creates steam and can toughen the meat.

GRATER GARLIC

For bigger garlic flavour on steak without burning it, slice garlic thinly and smear onto steak and leave there as it comes to room temperature. Scrape off before cooking but save and tip back into the grill-pan juices after the steak is removed. Cook quickly without browning and pile onto the steak.

LADLE MEATBALLS

Make small, even meatballs by pushing a pasta ladle into minced meat mixture and scooping off the amount that pops through the hole in the middle.

FLAVOUR STAKES

Season steak with salt and pepper only after cooking and while resting.

Dribble on excellent extra-virgin olive oil or add a knob of flavoured butter after cooking and while resting.

CHOP OR FORK

When you don't have a rack small enough to fit into a roasting pan, criss-cross chopsticks or inverted large forks to keep your ribs, roasts or birds off the base.

NO SPLAT

Lessen cleaning up splattered fat by covering unused burners or elements during cooking with an easily cleaned metal baking tray or secured kitchen foil.

COOL HOT STUFF

WHAT'S THE DIFFERENCE BETWEEN CHILLI AND CHILI—OR CHILE?

Chilli and chillies with two 'l's rhymes with Hell, a reminder these are Hotter than Hell, and that these are the proper words for the fruit, whatever its size, colour or heat. Chilli powder should mean only ground chillies.

Chili with one 'l' should mean a cooked dish containing chillies, such as chili con carne. Chile is a variation of chili.

Chili dishes are often fiery but otherwise banal because ground chillies have been mis-labelled and used instead of big-flavoured chili compound or powder.

Chili powder or compound should include cumin, oregano and garlic. That's the right, robust flavouring for a chili. Or a chile. Add other spices like turmeric or coriander and it becomes a curry.

WHERE'S THE FIRE?

The pale inner ribs of a chilli have most of the heat from capsaicin oil and the seeds have almost none.

A purple blush in the ribs indicates a high heat value.

Easiest removal/control is to slice from top to bottom and then remove both ribs and seeds with a sharp melon baller.

It's worth wearing rubber gloves.

BEER AND WATER DON'T QUENCH CHILLI OR CHILI HEAT

If your mouth is too hot, absorb chilli oils with rice or bread, otherwise, eat another fat, like milk, cheese, soured cream, yoghurt or butter, which will combine with and dilute the chilli oil. Drinking water, beer or wine flushes the chilli oils directly into your stomach and bowels and then …

ADDICTION RESULTS

Capsaicin oil in chillies burns the tongue, which the brain registers as injury and so it creates feel-good serotonins. That feeling is equivalent to a drug-high and explains why so many experience chilli-hot food as gratifying, whatever it tastes like.

Like all euphoria-producing drugs, the more you consume chillies, the more you need to equal the first sensation, BUT you have been creating scars on your tongue, which hide apparent damage, so you need increasingly more and more but taste less and less.

Using more chillies is common as palates age, but you are further blinding your tongue to the full pleasures of food, of fine wines, great whiskies, opulent ports and yes, even bread, butter, tea and coffee. Or cake.

IT'S NOT SO HOT ABROAD

Don't think it is authentic to copy the chilli-heat you experience abroad. That level of heat is NOT what the locals' life-long damaged tongues experience, so you are right to ask for or to use less.

TASTE TIPS

Replace chilli with strong explosions of flavour:

Very coarse black pepper

Roasted black peppercorns

Zest of lemons, limes or oranges

Roasted cumin seeds

Ground cumin

Cubes of acidic aged cheese

Fresh rocket

Fresh watercress leaves

Salt-preserved lemons

9

IN A STEW

KNOT FULL

Learn how to tie a butchers' knot, so you can make beef, pork and other roasts neatly shaped and thus cook evenly—you'll find many other ways to use this skill. Practise on a wine bottle, jam jar or can.

Slip string under the meat with a longer length on top and a shorter one protruding underneath.

Hold the two lengths between the thumb and forefinger of your left hand with the long one on top.

Loop the shorter length from under the meat under, over and back across the long length and then through the hole that is created. Pull the long length to tighten. Add another loop or knot for extra security.

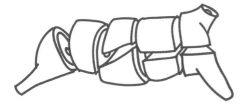

BROWN STUDY

Brown meat for stewing with no flour to get maximum colour and flavour; browning with seasoned flour mainly colours the flour and that adds little useful flavour.

FLOUR POWER

Stir flour for thickening a stew into the precooked vegetables you are adding, like properly browned onions or leeks: at least a tablespoon per litre of liquid for a medium to thin texture.

BROWNED NOT BURNED

It takes 40–45 minutes for 500 g/1 lb of onions to sweeten in butter or oil over very low heat. Turn up the heat now and the onions caramelise adding true heritage flavour.

Brown before they have sweetened and you carbonise, so curries, stews and casseroles will never taste like grandma made— she knew to put the onions on and then to walk away.

SWEETENING

Sweeten onions faster in the microwave. Cooked covered, with no added oil, butter or fat, which makes them more likely to burn.

SIZE MATTERS

Cut meat for stews at least 50% bigger than you want on the plate, as cooking shrinks meat and thus looks mean when served.

CONNECTIONS

Choose meat for stews that has connective tissue and gristle rather than fat-free single muscles, as these are what give voluptuous mouth feel. Chuck and shin and brisket are best and the combination of any of these is recommended.

EXPENSIVE NOT

Avoid single muscle meats for stewing, like rump or sirloin. Whatever you do, they will always be dry in the mouth.

MIXING IT

Make a mixture of chuck and shin for the most succulent stews. Using just one of these is good but not as good.

BULB LIGHT

Lighten *and* darken garlic content by cooking a whole unpeeled bulb of garlic in a stew, prepared by slicing off enough of the top to expose the individual cloves. The dish will be lighter in garlic than if you added the same amount peeled and chopped.

For those who want more, squash the custardy garlic from the skins onto the plate.

WELL-RESTED MEAT

Rest meat after roasting, grilling, frying or barbecuing. Each method contracts flesh and forces juices towards the surface. Resting allows the flesh to relax and then to reclaim and reabsorb the moisture. If you don't rest meat, it will lose moisture when cut—a sure sign—and that means toughness and less flavour.

RESTING TIMES

No-one expects meat to be boiling hot and roasted meat and poultry stays hotter than you think, giving plenty of time for cooking sauces and vegetables without fuss or rush.

Turkey or goose will still be very hot 45 minutes after it comes from the oven.

Rest steaks and chops in a warm not hot place for 10 minutes or more.

Roasts can wait 30 minutes or more.

So can chickens.

Rest game birds for 10–15 minutes.

MOIST TESTS

Rest meat roasts and roasted birds long enough so you do not see steam rising when you first carve, as this moisture should have been absorbed.

Making a puddle of liquid when cutting or carving means you have done this too soon.

NEVER FOILED AGAIN

Never cover cooked meats and poultry with a tent of foil because you create a steamy atmosphere and if water drips back it will dissolve flavour and soften any crispness.

Foil tents are an unnecessary modern expense invented by foil manufacturers. We managed without foil in castles to cottages for thousands of years.

HAMBURGERS AT HOME

Make even-sized patties (and fish cakes, too) by shaping with a biscuit/cookie cutter or in a deep screw-top lined with cling film.

Put chips of ice in the middle of a hamburger patty to keep the centre pink while you grill burger-brown outside.

Toast and generously butter hamburger buns—that's the original way. Floury, chewy bap-style buns work better than the soft sweet ones from burger chains.

STACK 'EM HIGH

Understand what made the original hamburgers so popular by stacking the buttered, toasted buns with plenty of lettuce (crunchy iceberg is favourite), plus modern caramelised grilled tomato rather than fresh, maybe roasted zucchini or red-pepper slices. And plenty of ketchup and mayo—aioli perhaps? And mild mustard or pickles— even a fruit chutney. In New Zealand, sliced beetroot is mandatory and sometimes grilled pineapple is, too.

MINCE MATTERS

Cook red-meat mince in a sauce a long time: it's made from tough cuts and so needs at least 45 minutes, longer is better. This includes meatballs particularly; a Bolognese sauce takes at least 90 minutes—*see opposite for the crush test*.

FLAVOUR SMELLS

Prepare mince by first frying with nothing else until it has lost all excess moisture and is starting to brown. It then smells of its origins, beef, pork, or lamb, and that dryness means each morsel will then absorb whatever flavours you add as stocks, sauces, finely chopped onion, herbs and spices and so on.

CRUSH TEST

Test a morsel of cooked mince against the roof of your mouth with just tongue pressure. It will disintegrate when properly tender.

DIFFERENT COURSES

Surprise by serving Yorkshire Puddings as puddings. Bake them over a little stewed fruit: rhubarb or apples are particularly good. Sprinkle with sugar before serving and then put ice cream into the hollow. Think of them as crisp, misshapen pancakes.

10

THE VEGGIE WAYS

Judge for yourself the advantages and myths about cooking vegetables.

MICROWAVING

This is optimal for flavour and health benefits, even Government websites say so. Fresh or frozen, the microwave steams away some of a vegetable's internal moisture, concentrating its goodness and flavour—no essentials are dissolved and wasted into cooking water. Add a little water only when cooking a large amount of root vegetables.

As we age and our taste buds diminish in ability, the microwave rewards us with greater flavour as well as important better nutrition. It's safer, too, especially in older households; no pans of boiling water and the microwave obediently turns itself off.

Anyone who says microwaves take the life out of vegetables has overcooked them or incorrectly microwaved them in water. Probably both.

ROASTING AND GRILLING

Increasingly popular, roasted or grilled vegetables offer excellent nutritional values plus the added bonuses of concentrated flavour and some caramelisation. Do this faster and save energy by first lightly microwaving and then tossing in a little oil before putting into the oven or under a grill.

STEAMING IN BAMBOO

When food is steamed in bamboo baskets Asian-style, it sits on a plate or round of paper in the basket. The bamboo absorbs most water vapour, so little or nothing condenses and then falls onto the food to dissolve flavour and nutrition on its way back into the boiling water. Any that does is collected on the plate or paper. A very close second to microwaving.

Note that flavouring steaming water is pointless as steam does not carry flavours.

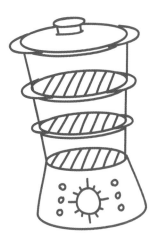

STIR-FRYING

Any liquid in stir-fried recipes is served with the dish and so stir-frying is very close to both microwaving and bamboo-steaming in the nutrition it returns.

STEAMING IN METAL

The Western way of steaming in and on metal is little better nutritionally than boiling, except for texture. Water vapour condenses inside the lid, falls back onto the food, dissolves the invaluable vitamins and flavour compounds and then drains these into the steaming liquid—easily seen and smelled. Great if you use that liquid, but most people do not.

BOILING

Nutrition and flavour are seriously compromised by being dissolved into the water. Compare the taste of a boiled vegetable and a properly microwaved one and you will astonish yourself at how lively the latter is.

11

VEGETABLES MATTER

SUN SINS

Sunlight speeds up the deterioration of harvested vegetables, yes, even organically grown. This is why markets and open displays outside shops are not that good an idea unless the produce is shaded. And this is why supermarket vegetables can be a better choice nutritionally, especially if also chilled.

CORNY WORDS

Judge sweetcorn cobs are ripe when the silk tassels at the top have turned red-brown.

Cook corn cobs in their outer husk leaves for best flavour whether boiling, grilling, microwaving or barbecuing, but first, pull them back, remove the silk, and then stroke the husks back into place.

Remove the silk with a light bristle brush or by wrapping rubber bands around your fingers and brushing with that.

Remember fresh corn gets less sweet the longer it has been picked and tougher the longer you cook it. Native Americans walked to collect corn cobs but ran home to cook them.

COOL CUCUMBER

Poach arcs of cucumber to look like jade:

→ Peel and slice a cucumber in half lengthwise, then scoop out the seeds using a teaspoon. Cut evenly into semi-circles about 2 cm/¾" wide and poach a few minutes until you see a slight colour change and then run under very cold water and they will turn transparent.

→ Use cold in salads, serve hot with butter or in a cream sauce, the way Georgians and Victorians did.

→ Poach thin slices until softening, cool completely in running water until bright green and translucent; use these to decorate a skinned, poached salmon or trout. Aspic to cover.

ONION CHOPS

Easiest way to chop onion is to peel it, cut a thin slice from the bottom so it sits neatly and then cut across the radius almost to the base a few or many times, according to the size of chopped onion you want. Then, slice in half, top to bottom, sit on a flat side and slice down, again according to the size you want.

TEARLESS ONIONS

Putting an onion into the freezer for 10–15 minutes will reduce its ability to cause tears.

PERKY PEPPERS

Keep stuffed peppers upright when baking by standing in large muffin tins.

SKINNY DIPPING

Tomatoes, peaches and other fruits will skin more easily if you cut a cross on their bottoms before covering with boiling water.

WIN ONE

One spear of microwaved broccoli has the nutrition of five cooked by boiling or steaming. Excellent way to trick kids who think they've won by eating only one.

SLAW RIDES

For finely sliced cabbage, cut in half and then use a vegetable peeler for thinner, even strips for coleslaw, salad or pickled cabbage.

SAUCY BEINGS

Ban 3-bean salads but do puree one can of beans with olive oil and feta cheese to make a sauce for another colour of beans: pureed chick peas surrounding red or black kidney beans perhaps.

VEGETABLE BUBBLES

Reboil vegetable stews containing unpeeled vegetables, like ratatouille, after 24 hours, which is the only way to kill yeasts that develop since the first cook; otherwise they will ferment and spoil the dish.

NOT ANY OLD RICE

Look for aged basmati rice, the only rice that improves by the year. Specialist suppliers have as many vintages and styles as a vintner. Cook by the absorption method or the nuances of flavour will be thrown out with the cooking water.

BARLEY PARLEY

Cook barley as a pilaff instead of rice:

→ Roast or fry in butter or oil until golden then cook with three parts stock or water to one of barley.

→ Great with fattier roasts and super with game birds.

OVER-BAKED POTATOES

Get more pleasure from baked potatoes by over baking them, creating a thick, crisp and savoury skin. Pierce but do not oil or butter the skins, as that can prevent crispness. After an initial burst in the microwave, bake at 200°C/400°F/gas 6 or more for at least an hour.

Cut them almost in half the second they come from the oven or the skin will soften, essential advice for all baked potatoes.

BEAN POISONED

Boil soaked red-kidney beans hard for at least 10 minutes during cooking or they are toxic. It's best to do the same to all dried kidney beans but canned ones are safe to eat as they are with no further heating.

BLOW OFF WINDS

Never cook soaked beans or lentils in water in which they have been soaked, because the wind-producing elements are still in full force.

SALT SENSE

Don't add salt or salted meats when cooking soaked beans until after they are tender. Doing so keeps the skins tough.

OLD SALTS

Accept that tongues become less sensitive with age. Using chilli or mustards to create mouth-feel increases the problem—*see Cool Hot Stuff on pages 47–48* for better ideas.

SALTING MYTHS

Salt does not change food and 'bring out the flavour'. Salt stimulates taste buds to taste more fully, but as each person has a different number of taste buds, Super-Tasters need no salt and Slow-Tongues need a lot to get the same taste but risk tasting more salt than food.

It is impossible to tell another mouth how much salt it needs.

BITTER LESSONS

Balance bitterness in food or drink with acidity, as in using lemon in harsh black tea. Sweetness has no counter-active effect on bitterness.

BAG AND BOTTLE

Keep cut herbs and all greens fresh and crisp for ages by sprinkling lightly with water, then putting them into a large freezer bag (a plastic carrier bag for large amounts).

Invert in the refrigerator with plenty of space within to create a hydrating atmosphere. Works better and for longer than storing cut herbs in water.

Store smaller amounts in screw-top bottles.

GREEN REFRESHMENT

Refresh tired green salads leaves, spinach, cabbage or other leafy vegetables by sprinkling lightly with water and storing for at least 30 minutes as above.

INSTANT SPAIN

Purée frozen ratatouille to make an instant gazpacho soup: if it's too thick purée in canned tomatoes and/or peeled cucumbers. Extra olive oil of course.

DEFROST COLD

Defrosting food in a dish or bowl slows the process as cold air is trapped by the container. For faster results, stand on a rack or flat plate.

CHUTNEY AND PICKLE SOURCES

Make chutney with fully ripe fruit: make pickles with barely ripe vegetables.

Choose any vinegar that is at least 5% acetic acid; sweeten with dark or white sugars.

Grind in spices for darker results; tie whole spice in muslin for a lighter colour.

Leave chutney and pickles at least two weeks before using—and as long as two years.

SALAD DAZE

Make old-fashioned salad cream for potato or other salads by whisking as you add in order: 1 egg, 400 g (approx.) sweetened condensed milk, 1 tsp mustard powder, 75 ml milk and 60 ml white wine, cider or tarragon vinegar. Leave to thicken for 10–20 minutes. Add capers, horseradish—whatever.

12

PASTA PECULIARS

DUMP THEM

Add gnocchi to meat or vegetable stews to make mini-dumplings. Cook no longer than recommended or they disintegrate.

DULLER IS BETTER

Find dull-looking pasta that has a rough texture you can sense with your teeth, like natural pearls. That's because it's been extruded and shaped traditionally through bronze dies, leaving a coarse surface. Seek the word *bronzato* or similar on packs.

The rougher surface of bronze-extruded pasta absorbs more of any sauce or dressing, combining the two before it gets to your mouth. Shiny pasta extruded through plastic can't do this.

HOLEY PASTA

The hole in a pasta server is the perfect measure for a single serving of dry spaghetti.

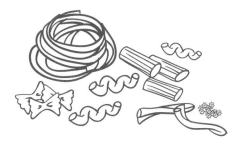

NON-STICK PASTA

If your pasta sticks together after cooking it's because you have not cooked it in enough water. Dried pasta absorbs 1½ times its volume of water, so a ratio of 1 litre of rapidly boiling water to 100 g dried pasta is a minimum and much more is better; increase the water proportionally for more pasta. Salt very well.

CALM WATERS

Adding oil to pasta cooking water does not solve the sticky problem. A touch of oil is added to prevent foam spilling out of the pot and this is where the confusion began. Cook in plenty of water to prevent pasta sticking together; oil on water does not do it.

SAUCING TIME FOR PASTA

Wait a few minutes before saucing cooked and drained pasta until most steam has stopped rising, which means the rough surfaces of bronze-extruded pasta (and to a lesser degree the smoother surfaces of plastic-extruded types) have dried and will then absorb much more sauce.

Do this naturally when drained pasta is piled on to a serving plate and the sauce is added to the middle but mixed only when served at the table.

THAT PASTA COOKING-WATER THING ...

Forget the idea of stirring pasta-cooking water into a pasta sauce. Nowhere in Italy does this as a matter of course, except if a regional sauce has reduced too much, which is unlikely because thicker is better. Wouldn't you rather add more of an ingredient already there rather than diluting with salty, floury water?

GETTING IN TO SHAPE

Choose a pasta shape according to the sauce:

→ Rugged, lumpy sauces with bits of vegetable, seafood or meat are best with shaped pasta, so there are cavities and folds and tubes to hold the pieces as you catch them on your fork.

→ Smooth pastas like fettucine and spaghetti were created to go with smoother sauces and work much better with bronze-extruded pasta that has been allowed to steam dry before being mixed with the sauce—some will be absorbed into the pasta rather than puddling on the plate.

Shapes that are both basically smooth but are hollow tubes can do both, like penne.

Ridged or grooved shapes can do for most sauces, especially grooved penne rigata or bigger penne regine.

MAC 'N' PIZZA

Pimp macaroni cheese by baking it topped with everything except the crust that makes a favourite pizza: tomato, mozzarella, salami, black olives, olive oil, dried oregano, whatever. Outstanding outdoor food, hot or cold. Fabulous for fireworks.

13

MICROWAVE MARVELS

Think of your microwave as a steamer and you'll never be disappointed with floppy results—it can't do crisp unless it's vegetables, spices and nuts.

MICROWAVE BASICS

Microwaves work in the presence of water, oil and sugar and the more there is of one or all, the faster they work.

Microwaves penetrate about 2.5 cm/1 inch according to density. They do not cook from the inside out but cook the penetrated thickness all at once:

other methods rely on the heat being transferred from the outer surface.

Recommend a microwave for the kitchen of older cooks, because it is obedient, safely switching off when told to do so.

VEGGIE STUFF

Vegetables are cooked in a microwave by the steam-heat of the water they contain; as this is released it concentrates the flavour and nutrition.

Cook vegetables, including frozen vegetables, with no added water but covered with pierced or folded back cling film. The exception is large quantities of root vegetables, especially potatoes, but only add a little water.

Or cover food to be microwaved with a plate, serving side down, and when it's ready you'll have a hot plate to use.

Frozen vegetables are processed within hours of harvesting, giving a freshness nothing in shops or supermarkets can equal. Sometimes the varieties frozen are not the best tasting but the superior nutrition is always there.

BAN BACON SCUM

Cook bacon slices between absorbent kitchen paper in the microwave and never see excess moisture, scum or fat again. Works even better with dry-cured bacon, quickly giving crisp, golden fat.

Timing depends on thickness of bacon and microwave power, so start slowly.

MORE MICRO-HACKS

Cook porridge in minutes, while you are in the shower— it won't boil over or burn unless instructed to do so.

Roast nuts without added oil. They cook all through for greater flavour and texture; arrange in a circle on a plate, cook uncovered in bursts of a minute or more, mixing and rearranging from time to time. Life changing.

Peel and roast chestnuts marvellously: cut a cross through the pointed top of each and microwave six to eight for a few minutes until you see the cross opening. Allow to cool a little while you process the next batch. They peel best when still warm, hence the small batch method.

Micro-roast black peppercorns as above, a little or a lot. Doubles your repertoire, giving extra depths of flavour to everything from eggs and sandwiches to curries and stews.

Micro-roast cumin seeds and use as sprinkles to add texture and flavour bursts to salads, sandwiches, roasted or grilled vegetables, cheeseboards and more.

Heat curry powders and masalas with no added oil for cleaner, clearer flavours.

Make best-ever mashes faster by microwaving starchy potato in chunks with a few tablespoons of water (the only time you do this). Remove the film and the potatoes are ready to mash—no need to dry them further.

NOTHING STEAMY

One of the greatest ways to make Christmas Day and Christmas pudding even more welcome is to banish steamy Christmas kitchens by microwaving your pudding on the day. Nine minutes at Medium is the same as two hours of steaming over water for the average pudding size. Most bought ones have microwave steaming times if you look and home-made ones do just as well.

Microwave other steamed puddings to save hours and eliminate steamy kitchens.

BUTTERING FAVOUR

Brandy and rum butters should not be served with Christmas pudding; they are meant to go with mince pies.

SAUCY I

Best and most traditional sauce for Christmas
pudding is a light vanilla custard, made
lump-free in the microwave, flavoured with
orange zest and/or a splash of such as Cointreau,
Triple Sec, Grand Marnier or Mandarine
Napoleon, but be creative.

———

SAUCY II

Make thickened sauces, custards and more
in the microwave faster and with no lumps.

———

SAUCY III

Microwave a caramel sauce
in minutes, but with care:

Put sweetened condensed milk in a deep bowl
and microwave a minute at a time—there's so much fat,
sugar and water it happens very fast.
Watch without fail, whisking after every minute or so,
being careful to keep your fingers away from
the sauce. Depending on the power you use, this can take
only a few minutes or up to ten, each one of them rewarded.

Make it more voluptuous by stirring in cream or salted butter.

Be cool and when it's well cool, stir in salt flakes
(like Maldon) or muscular crystals to make proper salted
caramel—you have to be able to taste salt or it's just caramel.

When almost cold, stir in roughly chunked dark
chocolate or/and micro-roasted nuts.

———

14

WOK'S WHAT

SHAPING UP

Pre-heat woks until smoking without oil or any other ingredients. This also helps build a non-stick surface.

Stir-fry using the entire wok surface because it heats evenly all over.

That's because a wok's shape is the form that sheet metal takes naturally when placed directly over flames, as also seen in the Indian Karahi.

It is impossible to get the correct amount and style of heat over a normal domestic gas flame unless you are cooking for one. If cooking substantially for two or more you are likely to be stewing rather than stir-frying, so should use something flat bottomed.

Get true wok-burn flavour by:

→ Fiercely heating the wok completely empty and

→ Lightly pre-cooking ingredients in the microwave, so they are hot all through when added. Many an Asian cook living out of their home country knows this.

Add flavouring liquids to a hot wok by pouring them around the wok above the food, so they run down evenly. This ensures they are hot before being stirred into the ingredients and are incorporated evenly.

Preserve your wok's non-stick surface by rinsing quickly while still hot, using no detergent or soap, and then wiping dry.

SMOKING THE WOK

Smoking food in a wok is an ancient Chinese thing to do and is a wondrous way to add flavour and excitement without having to own a smoking hut. It can be used two ways:

→ Hot-smoking, which cooks food at the same time as it smokes. Fish is the best choice, especially such oily ones as mackerel and salmon.

→ Flavour smoking, which adds a smoked finish to already-cooked food, including duck or chicken breasts, belly of pork, ham or bacon joints, sausages, and vegetables including baby potatoes, thick sliced sweet potatoes or squash and tomatoes. It's a great joke to smoke shelled, hard-boiled eggs because they look as though they still have brown shells and no-one knows until they pick them up, and then drop them because they are soft.

Start by lining a wok and its cover with foil, shiny side up. Then mix together 125 g/4 oz rice or barley with 50 g/2 oz of black tea leaves, which can be very ordinary, so use nothing special or scented. Put that mixture into the base of the lined wok.

Add a metal rack and put the food on that, leaving plenty of space for smoke to circulate.

Put the lid on tightly. Wet a couple of tea towels, wring

them out and then twist them. Use these to seal the wok; the smoke smells delicious but is permeating and will make everything smell if it escapes.

For Hot-smoking:

→ Put the sealed wok over maximum heat for ten minutes. For big amounts of food and food in big pieces, reduce the heat to low for another five minutes. For food in small pieces, remove from heat after ten minutes. In both cases, leave sealed for at least ten minutes, to allow the smoke to settle. You can leave the wok sealed up to an hour and the food will still be warm and moist.

For Flavour-smoking:

→ Put the sealed wok over maximum heat for ten minutes and then remove and let stand at least ten minutes.

The only thing you might do wrong is to over smoke and that's quickly learned. Counter act it by serving with something acidic, like soured cream or yoghurt, citrus juice or a dressing that includes vinegar.

Otherwise ignore versions that put sugar in the mix, which adds nothing but acridity. Neither does adding alcohol or herbs do anything detectable. However, a flavoursome sawdust or wood chips, such as camphor wood, sandalwood, hickory, cedar or manuka can substitute for a third of the tea leaves. Using only wood is likely to be too strong.

15

FRUIT PICKS

BERRY BEST FLAVOURS

Enjoy sweeter more fragrant strawberries, raspberries and blueberries by serving at room temperature. Store them in the refrigerator but remove well before you eat—you'll probably add less sugar too.

PROPER STRAWBERRIES AND CREAM

Recreate the old-fashioned way to enjoy strawberries and cream:

→ Cut hulled strawberries into halves or large chunks, and pour on cream that is thick and liquid or that has been whipped only until lollopy.

→ Add caster sugar, stir a couple of times and then leave an hour at room temperature, or four in the refrigerator but then allow to come back to ambient.

The cream and juices make a pinky-streaky sauce and the flavour seems to double.

Disturb the streakiness as little as possible when serving but keep puddling when you eat.

A little orange-flower water, rose water or jasmine essence adds aromatic magic. So does finely chopped preserved ginger. Or a little of a liqueur mentioned below.

THE HULL STORY

If you must wash strawberries, do this before hulling, that is removing the green top, or you risk dissolving some of the juices and flavour.

MUSH-FREE MARINADES

Macerate strawberries and other berries only in a liquid thicker than their natural juices; soaking in thinner wine or orange juice dilutes berries' natural juices and results in slushy berries with mushy skins but sweet liqueurs or dessert wines have the texture that avoids this.

Slightly sugar strawberries and then add only enough wine, orange juice, champagne or liqueur to make a clingy syrup. An hour at room temperature or much longer in the refrigerator, and then add a little more of the liquid just before serving if you must.

LIQUEURS FOR STRAWBERRIES

Choose these liqueurs to drink with, to marinate or to flavour cream for strawberries: Cointreau or Grand Marnier (orange), Crème de Cacao (chocolate), Parfait d'Amour (vanilla-ish), Cassis (blackcurrant), Frangelico (hazelnut), Galliano (vanilla-herbal) and white or green Crème de Menthe (mint).

BRANDIED FRUITS

Use intense, unsweetened fruit brandy (*eau de vie*) very discreetly to punch up fruit desserts at the last minute. *Poire Williams* on raspberries; *framboise* on grilled peaches, *Calvados* on baked pears or apples or on a Tarte Tatin.

FRUIT PUDDLES
Grill or bake pear, peach or nectarine halves in which there is a little dark sugar. Before serving, add a puddle of sweet liqueur *framboise* (raspberry) or *Poire William* to pears, *fraises des bois* (wild strawberries) to white peaches/nectarines. Etc.

BLACK IS BACK
Pep up strawberries with freshly ground black pepper. It works. With sugar, of course.

MINT-FRESH
Mint mingles excellently with strawberries, fresh or as crème de menthe, especially in cream, in ice creams and mousses and in berry marinades. So good in a sorbet.

MIDDLE-EAST FLORAL MAGIC
Make raspberries taste even more of themselves with splashes of rose water, distilled from fresh roses. Use discreetly, especially in a freshly sieved coulis; raspberry with rose water is one of the best sauces for strawberries. Ever.

Enhance strawberries spectacularly with orange-flower water, distilled from orange blossom, especially in accompanying cream or sprinkled on with a little sugar.

DOUBT THE DOUBTERS
Think of roses when you taste rose water, not soap. Unsophisticated palates often describe rose water as tasting like soap. Wrong. Soap is hoping to emulate roses and rose water - and usually comes off badly. Such a sensual ingredient.

FAMILY FAVOURITES
Boost apple pies and sauces with a little rose water. Apples and roses belong to the same family, and so reliably give a genuine heritage flavour, especially with a buttery pastry and extra butter plus cinnamon on the sliced apples. It's what Shaker communities used to bake.

STRAWBERRY FAVOURS

Favour strawberries with red rather than pink or white flesh, for these are the tastiest. Autumn is traditionally a good time for them but supermarket favourite Murano is a summer bonanza, as is the more delicate but wondrous Mara des Bois, which has wild strawberries in its genetics.

BIRD-FREE STRAWBERRIES

Grow the creamy-white and intensely aromatic variety of small, Alpine 'wild' strawberries, *fragraria Vesca*. Birds ignore them, so you get the full crop. Just a few will scent a fruit salad if you let it sit awhile.

RASPBERRY SURPRISE

Rely on the surprising culinary friendship of raspberries and pears. Raspberry coulis with pears, *framboise eau de vie* on grilled pear halves, or pearly pear sorbet with nuggets of raspberry sorbet to mine inside.

RHUBARB SHAPES

Keep rhubarb's shape and better tastes by cooking without added

liquid. Then, stir it into strands if you want and they will not be watery.

Roasted, microwaved or in a saucepan, cut into big chunky lengths, sprinkled with sugar and cooked gently until tender.

Top results come from cooking with orange zest, chopped preserved stem ginger or darkest muscovado sugar.

Adding fresh mint is more original, especially for ice cream.

Top your muesli, add to yoghurts, make a fool or an ice cream.

Use the firm chunks or strips for a Millennial-style deconstructed Rhubarb Crumble—*see page 23.*

REMEMBER THIS?

Blend rhubarb and strawberries to make a very old country-style combination, giving a spectrum of flavour from acid to sweet. Works well in ice cream, or make rhubarb crumble and serve with proper strawberries and cream—*see above.*

BANANA-NO

When a banana is ripe, the skin makes no noise as it is peeled.

A greener, more bitter-tasting banana is better for colon health and helps absorb calcium, if you can stand the noise.

CURTAINS FOR JAM

Test if jam or marmalade is at setting point with a wooden spoon or spatula.

Tip so the edge is pointing down and the liquid can run off.
It's done if the jam collects and creates a curtain before dropping, rather than dripping off in blobs. Yes, there are other ways but this works.

FLOATING JAM FRUIT

Wait to bottle for 10 to 15 minutes after cooking jam or marmalade, which allows the mixture to settle and distribute fruit and peel evenly.

Stand hot, recently filled jam jars on their lids if fruit or peel floats to the top. You might have to turn them several times as they cool before you get even distribution.

If the tops and lids are not absolutely clean you will have trouble opening the jars.

SHARP PRACTICE

Get more citrus juice these ways:

→ Roll a lemon or other juice fruit on a firm surface, which breaks down inner membranes.

→ Microwave until warm but not hot.

→ Cut into quarters rather than halves when using a citrus press.

CITRUS TIPS

Cut off the end of a lemon, lime or orange when you want only a small amount of juice, rather than halving. Squeeze through the hole and then seal that with cling film.

16

PUDDING IT RIGHT

DESERT DESSERT

Soak mixed, dried fruit in orange, apple or pineapple juice, with or without a few teaspoons of orange flower water; in the Middle East, where this is called *koshaf*, they would use just water but these are better. Leave 24 hours or more at room temperature or two days in the refrigerator, turning lightly from time to time. The fruit will swell and their sugars exchange to make a syrup—leave at room temperature longer if this has not happened.

Eat small amounts, with or without buttery or gingery biscuits. A perfect snack to have in the refrigerator at Christmas and other holidays.

Bake in or under pastry in a pie: layer with clotted or whipped cream in millefeuilles or eclairs.

SIMPLE ICE CREAM

Create an infallible ice cream faster and that doesn't need to be beaten while freezing. Whisk together approximately even volumes of VERY cold sweetened condensed milk and double (heavy) cream: a 397 g of condensed milk and 300 ml of cream or a 170 g tube of condensed milk and 150 ml cream. It will thicken almost as much as whipped cream alone.

Flavour with vanilla or other extracts, or with the ideas below: alcohol will inhibit freezing.

RE-FLAVOUR ICE CREAM

Melt ice cream slightly and then quickly swirl in something wonderful; serve at once or refreeze. Don't mix enthusiastically or you will lose the air in the ice cream. Try:

→ Lightly crushed raspberries and/or strawberries with a little sugar, orange juice liqueur or flower water.

→ Frozen Fruits of the Forest mixture.

→ Frozen tropical fruit mixes meant for smoothies—chop smaller.

→ Crumbled Christmas cake or pudding, moistened with a very little sherry, rum or brandy; good in chocolate or coffee ice cream as well as in vanilla.

→ Chopped nut brittle, peppermint rock, liquorice all-sorts.

→ Turn cornflakes in butter and brown sugar, cool, crumble and mix in.

ICE-CREAM SCOOP

Forget the interminable faff of freezing hands while scooping individual ice-cream portions. And always have an individual serving ready.

Divide almost frozen home-made ice cream into muffin or cup-cake papers. Freeze on flat trays or in muffin/cupcake trays. Save space when frozen by wrapping individually in cling

CRÊPES!
Make pancakes thick and crêpes thin.

film and storing in a zip-lock freezer bag.

Pre-portion bought ice cream by softening only slightly, then proceeding as above.

Make both special with a little fruit or chocolate sauce at the bottom of each—or some microwave caramel—*see page 75.*

WHITE OUT
Remember white chocolate is not really chocolate because it is the fat expressed from cacao pods and includes no cocoa solids.

SUCK IT AND SAVE
Freeze chocolate in (big) bite-sized squares; suck a piece when you crave chocolate and then it takes long enough to melt on the tongue for you to feel you have eaten much more.

SAUCY CREAMS
Strain creamy sauces, including custard, through a sieve for smoother textures.

FLAT SCOOPS
Flatten the top of each scoop of ice cream against the pack or other surface, and, when it is released onto pie, pudding or cake, it won't slide off.

PIED MERINGUES
Spread meringue mixture right to the edges when topping a pie or it will shrink and weep.

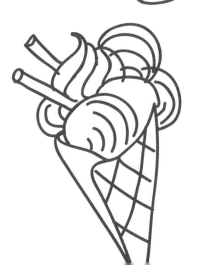

17

CHEF STUFF

TASTING THE DIFFERENCE

Know the difference between 'tastes' and 'flavours'.

Tastes are correctly only sweet, sour/acidic, salt, bitter and umami.

Everything else is flavour, a combination of these tastes plus many other aromatics.

We complicate this by saying we 'taste' food but that verb is a confusion, because you are tasting flavours as well as tastes. Got it?

TASTE DIRECTIONS

Work out how your tongue registers tastes by remembering which part of the tongue is most likely to taste what. Although most of the mouth registers all tastes, we are more likely to get a stronger reaction in particular areas.

SUGAR: the tongue's most sensitive area for detecting sweetness is at the tip of the tongue.

SALT: most likely to be tasted on the side of the tongue.

ACID: towards the sides of the tongue.

BITTER: at the back of the tongue, a final warning before swallowing, because many bitter foods are also poisonous.

UMAMI: the savoury taste is experienced in most parts of the mouth.

Eating must gratify the mouth before it does the stomach. We chew to mix in saliva, an important pre-digestive aid. As that happens, our mouth should be flooded with sensation and flavour, gratification that sates mouth hunger. If mouth hunger is not satisfied, because you swallow too quickly, or if fats and oils insulate the tastebuds from taste and flavour, the mouth will crave more and so you eat more than the stomach needs to be satisfied.

The answer is only to eat foods that bite back with flavour – and then you'll eat less. Bite back does not mean chilli-hot food, which are as bad as bland, because the mouth has little chance to detect what else is there so you eat more than you truly need.

FEED BOTH HUNGERS

Understand why you eat more bland food than you need, and why you eat less of a food that bites back in the mouth yet gratifies both mouth hunger and stomach hunger.

THE CRUNCH

Use semolina for a crunchy crust to vegetables. Turn cooked potatoes in it lightly before putting into the hot roasting pan and do the same to oil-tossed vegetables you are about to roast.

HEADY RELIEF

Relieve summer headaches by including a sprig of fresh rosemary with tea brewing in a pot.

CHOP AND CHANGE

Chop parsley and other herbs without making a mess by snipping with scissors in a deep cup or mug.

Or use a pizza cutter on a board.

SOUP FIZZICALS

Pour a little sparkling wine or champagne into the middle of chilled soups just as you are serving, for super-chic foam without fuss.

MORE LEMON

Get more juice from lemons, oranges, limes and grapefruit by microwaving 10–20 seconds according to size; they should be warm rather than hot, which would change the flavour.

NO COTTAGE SHEPHERDS

Know the difference. Shepherd's pie should be minced lamb, and cottage pie should be beef. Both are made best with leftover roasted meat with plenty of gravy mixed through.

GREATER AS GRATINS

Bake any vegetable dish better with a gratin topping to finish. Sprinkle breadcrumbs evenly over cooked vegetables or vegetables in a sauce, with or without pasta included. Grate butter over the crumbs for a light flavour or sprinkle on olive oil for a Mediterranean twist. For something bolder, grate hearty cheese on to either or as a singular choice. Bake until heated through and the breadcrumbs are browned and crisp. Mix finely zested orange, lemon or lime peel, garlic or chopped herbs into the crumbs, too, especially fresh coriander, which keeps much of its tang.

TOASTED ENOUGH

Get enough toast under your eggs, your baked beans, your full English. Toast two slices, cut them diagonally and then arrange the four pieces with the pointed ends meeting in the middle—a plate of toast.

MELBA SINGS

Make your own thin Melba-style toast. Toast slices the usual way and when cool split horizontally. Reverse these, so the toasted sides are together, the uncooked sides now outside, and toast again like this.

FRIED RIGHTS

Make tastier fried rice by spreading cooked rice to dry on a baking tray, ideally overnight, so it will then absorb the soy sauces and other aromatic flavourings when frying.

BEST LADLE HACK IN THE BOOK

Use the bottom of a soup ladle in a sieve to strain or purée anything. It's much faster than the tiny tip of a wooden spoon, you can use more pressure and you get far greater yields. Brilliant time saver and more profitable, too.

COLD FACTS

Give the proper time to marinades for flavours to exchange and improve:

→ Ignore advice to put something to marinate in the refrigerator for an hour or so, as nothing will happen.

→ Calculate that one hour of flavour exchange at room temperature takes four hours in the refrigerator.

ZEST FOR

Zest lemon, lime or orange directly over and close to where you need the flavour or you lose the fine spray of oil that has most flavour.

Don't grate direct onto a chopping board as this absorbs the oils.

Harvest vital but usually wasted citrus oils after grating by rubbing the outside and inside of the grater with one of the dish's ingredients, such as flour from a mixture, and then incorporate.

CUBE IT

When you want citrus flavour but not the zest, perhaps when baking, scrub the rind of an orange, lemon or lime with a sugar cube and then crumble it to use.

HIGH SALT LEVELS

Salting by hand from a good height above food isn't cheffy show-off but ensures it falls evenly; salting too close can mean salty surprises.

GERM-FREE GARLIC

Avoid garlic-smelly chopping boards by sticking a garlic clove onto the point of a sharp knife. Pull away the skin and then flake the flesh finely with a vegetable peeler directly into or onto where you want. The thin slices melt into sauces and are less challenging when served raw in, say, a potato salad. Perfect start to true aioli.

You'll also slice around the central germ, avoiding its usual bitterness.

SQUARE UP TO PARMESAN

Cut Parmesan or Grana Padano or a great Cheddar into small cubes rather than grating, especially for pasta. Instead of it disappearing, it will constantly surprise the palate with full-flavour hits of what you have paid so much to enjoy.

CHEESE SAUCE

Reduce cooking liquids, especially from roasting chickens, and while warm whisk in Boursin garlic-and-herb cheese to make an immediate creamy sauce.

OIL-FREE SALADS

Eliminate the oil and taste more of the salad by tossing instead in a very little gin, which gives great mouth feel and a slight bite, too. A little lime or lemon zest adds spritz. Especially good on salad leaves used as garnish.

DASHING VERMOUTH

Keep a bottle of dry white vermouth handy. A dash or much more of its high herbal flavours instead of wine adds magical lifts to risotto and pilaffs, to vegetable dishes, fish sauces and cheese or pasta sauces.

THE ART OF THREE

Make any meal look unexplainably better by serving only odd numbers on the plate. One sandwich or three, but not two. Three or five ingredients in a salad, not four or six. Meat and two vegetables, not three, although a sauce can make up the odd number. The rule of three also works when arranging flowers, displaying objects, stacking books, planting out … everywhere.

POPPING WILD

Create new textures and tastes by popping wild rice. Heat a little oil in a heavy-based saucepan, swirl in wild rice, cover and leave over medium heat, shaking the pan from time to time. They won't pop as loudly as corn, or become cloud-like but will butterfly and swell a bit. Flavour lightly with salt, pepper, perhaps a garlic or herb butter. Great as a snack, or stirred into soup, and Canadians mix them into meat balls and call these porcupine.

SET IT RIGHT

Don't try to set fresh pineapple, papaya or kiwi fruit in gelatine because enzymes prevent this happening. Use only canned pineapple or papaya and forget kiwi fruit.

Vegans and vegetarians will find agar-agar has even more problems and won't set chocolate.

MILKING THE BAY

Flavour milk or cream with bay leaves, an old-fashioned taste that lifts runny or baked custards, ice cream, crème brûlée, even a trifle.

Excellent with baked apples, apple pie, summer berries and in a sophisticated trifle.

TEMPER, TEMPER

Stir more of any or all herbs and spices originally used into long-cooked curries, casseroles or stews just before serving to refresh and add savour. It's called tempering and that's the real purpose of garam masala.

GARAM MASALA

Use garam masala properly to temper spiced dishes, that is sprinkled on or stirred in at the last moment to refresh and enhance the differing flavours of cooked spices.

Use Western-style to create gentler dishes as it is fragrant and usually contains little chilli.

Give the mixture a quick burst in the microwave to release the fragrance of the spices without dulling or burning them in oil.

BOUQUET BALLS

Instead of tying fresh herbs for a bouquet garni, trap them in a tea-ball infuser. Great for crushed spices when tempering, as above.

HEATING CURRY

Heat spices before curry mixes and masala before fluids are added or they are added to something already cooking.

Fry in a little oil until the fragrance is released but it's less fuss to do this in the microwave.

It's what you should do before adding to rice for a kedgeree, to mayo for Coronation Chicken or to butch up a weakling curry.

SAFFRON SCENTS

Don't add saffron strands directly to cooking liquids, as you don't get full value. Pour on boiling water and let soak at least 30 minutes and then add both the strands and the brilliant brew.

BLACK PEPPER EXTRAS

It takes only five minutes of cooking for the bright and fragrant heat of freshly ground black pepper to oxidise and lose its virtues, so:

→ Stir freshly ground black pepper into hot dishes just before serving and it lifts fragrance and flavours magically.

→ Roast black peppercorns to double your culinary repertoire. The microwave does this best —*see page 73*—and you might make several caches, some lightly roasted, some darker. The complicated smoky flavours are transformational on everything from a tomato sandwich to smoked salmon, a chicken gravy to oxtail stew or a vegetable, vegetarian or vegan stir-fry. No new recipes to learn, just a new flavour to add to what you already do.

CHOCOLATE BITES

Add an intriguing square of dark chocolate per serving to any sauce rich in tomatoes and spices. This includes chili con carne. Be sparing, you might not need that much.

Use a little cocoa powder instead of chocolate to add to tomato and spice-based sauces but it will be bitter if you use too much.

Dutched cocoa dissolves more easily and is less bitter.

BAKED-BEAN CAN DO

Add a few slugs of rugged red wine to canned baked beans for extraordinary results. Let simmer a while.

Also add whole lightly crushed garlic cloves in their skin, a bay leaf, a dash of Worcestershire sauce—even chunks of meaty Polish or other cooked sausages, like chorizo. Grind on and stir through black pepper. With sourdough toast for breakfast or lunch, or bubbling beside a barbecue.

STOCK CONTENT

Speed up defatting of hot or warm stock by:

→ Dropping in ice cubes to which the fat will adhere.

→ Floating on pieces of kitchen paper, which absorbs the fat but leaves the stock.

SERRATING PASTRY

To cut filled pastries—custard squares or profiteroles—use either a serrated bread knife or, better, an electric knife and with almost no pressure. The filling won't end up as a border.

FILO STACKS

To get maximum crisp but light pastry layering, bake stacks of buttered or oiled filo-pastry shapes direct on a baking tray. Make individual serving sizes or big squares to sandwiches' hot fillings and take to table as Fly-Away Filo Pies, savoury or sweet.

EDIBLE BOWLS

Make small edible bowls for chili, mayonnaise salads or green salads by dipping the bottom of a soup ladle into pancake batter up to the rim, and then holding the ladle to the same level in hot oil until the shape is cooked and brown. Repeat.

Flavour the batter highly with spices, citrus zest or garlic if you don't mind it browned.

NEW PICKLES

Follow the trend and serve pickled vegetables and fruit the new way, lightly soaked in a fragrant vinegar or genuinely sharp verjuice. Slice them fresh and thinly and choose such special vinegars as chardonnay or champagne, cider or tarragon, sherry vinegar or extraordinary Pedro Ximinez, the richest, darkest of all, ideal for any fruit to serve with something chocolate. A couple of hours is maximum or you will ambush the fruit or vegetable flavour and compromise its texture.

LEFT IS RIGHT

Serve food on the left side of anyone seated, the professional way for centuries, so you do not risk knocking a wine glass or getting bumped by a diner reaching for wine.

BUT remove plates from the right side, when there is less risk of spillage. Reverse it for seated left handers.

POURING DOWN

Only pour wine on the right side of a diner, so you do not invade their space by putting an arm across them.

18

KITCHEN STUFF

SPACE MAKING

Put a chopping board over the sink to make more prep or serving surface available.

Create extra counter space by putting a chopping board over a pulled-out drawer BUT, do make sure the drawer is stable and not pulled out too far.

SECURITY MEASURES

Avoid annoying curling of cutting boards by standing on an edge to dry rather than lying flat.

Anchor an unsteady cutting board or mixing bowl by sitting it on a damp, folded cloth or cloths of the same dimensions.

Non-slip shelf lining paper can be used over and over.

NOT A THICKY

Avoid curdling when mixing liquids by always pouring the thicker into the thinner.

WOODEN YOU KNOW

Sweeten wooden chopping boards when rinsed and dry using one of two ways. First is to rub cut lemon onto the surface. Second is to make a paste of baking soda and water, leave for several hours and then rinse.

NON-STICK NO

Use a non-stick spray on non-stick pans and you risk creating a sludgy crust that is difficult to remove. Why would you?

UNSTICK YES

Remove a burnt-on crust in a saucepan by simmering hot water and a dishwasher tablet or boiling up with plenty of detergent.

CAN MUST DO

Clean off the dangerous food collected between the serrated disc and the cutting wheel of can openers to avoid potential for food poisoning. Drip on a little bleach and then run folded kitchen paper through the mechanism until clean and dry.

Or regularly put into the dishwasher.

SILVER SERVICE

Use kitchen foil and baking soda (bicarbonate of soda/sodium bicarbonate) to clean silver fuss-free and without metal loss:

Line a deep bowl or baking tray with kitchen foil dull side up, shake in a thick layer of baking soda; proportions are not exact but be generous. Put in silver spoons, forks, silver-handled knives making sure each on is touching the foil and then cover with very hot water. It will foam up at first but when subsided keep an eye out until the cutlery looks bright. Remove, rinse, dry and buff.

You might need to do it twice or double the amount of soda but the silver will not be damaged.

Big or complicated pieces should be wrapped in foil and covered with the above solution, perhaps in a deep bowl.

FLYING TACKLES

Tackle fruit-fly problems with a small bowl of honey, syrup or jam covered by cling film but with a slight amount folded back. The greedy pests will find their way in but not out. Or …

BASIL AMBUSH

Set a basil plant beside a fruit bowl to deter fruit flies and other problems.

Plant or pot plenty of basil close to outside eating areas and put a pot on the table to ambush all flying annoyances, including mosquitoes.

MORE SODA TO DO

Place a saucer of baking soda (sodium bicarbonate, bicarbonate of soda) in your refrigerator and it will absorb unwanted smells.

Sweeten tainted plastic storage containers by soaking in a strong baking soda solution.

TOOTHSOME SILVER

Use a dry toothbrush to remove dried cleaning powder from ornate silver. Please!

SILVER OCCASIONS

Wrap little-used silver or silver plate in cling film and it will not tarnish between uses.

SAUCY SHINES

Clean and polish copper or brass with ketchup, brown sauce or tomato sauce. Leave five minutes or so and then wipe off, rinse and shine.

Use baking soda (bicarbonate of soda, sodium bicarbonate) and a little water to remove small spots, rubbing with little pressure.

Or mix three parts of citrus juice, lemon ideally, to one part of salt. Apply with a soft cloth when the salt is dissolved.

Make a dip for big pieces with one-part vinegar to three parts water and two tablespoons of salt

to every litre of liquid. Boil this up and then dip.

COPPER MINDING

Apply a fine film of light oil to protect clean copper or brass.

CLEAR VIEWS

Combat and reverse cloudy glassware from the dishwasher in hard-water areas by using twice the amount of dishwasher liquid or tablets. The clouds are residual minerals left because the washing medium couldn't cope with the amount in the water.

BLOWING HOT AND COLD

Ignore temperature controls on your oven or ovens as they can vary up or down by 10 or more degrees. Buying an oven temperature gauge is the best guarantee of baking success.

SHARP PRACTICE

Protect your fingers and knives stored in drawers by inserting the tips into thick slices of used wine bottle corks or a blob of Blu Tack, children's modelling clay or plasticine. A wall-mounted magnetic rack is a better idea.

DRIP CONTROL

Avoid sticky olive and other oil bottles and unsightly labels caused by drips and drizzles by stretching a sweat band above the label. Easy to chuck into the washer when it gets dirty.

Stop jugs dripping after pouring, whether water, milk, sangria or juices, by putting a dab of butter or firm margarine on the lip, which will catch them before they fall.

JAMMED JARS

Open difficult jam, pickle and other jars the old-fashioned way by using a solid wooden door. Open the door widely and put the cap into the space between the door's edge and the frame. Close the door onto that as tightly as you can, and then twist the jar with your free hand. Keep the jar tilted up a little, to avoid sudden drips or floods. It might help first to run the cap under hot water.

GETTING A HANDLE

Rest your thumb along the top of a kitchen knife handle and pointing towards the tip. That's the professional way and gives more power and control than having your index finger there, which can get painful when it is flexed backwards if you press hard.

BLADE RUINERS

Stop slapping an expensive kitchen knife onto a steel sharpener while held horizontally, which can make dents in the blade or chip it. You tend also only to sharpen the central portion. Do what the best butchers do:

→ Hold a sharpening steel vertically for best sharpening, even better if the tip is firm on a tough surface or chopping board.

→ Start with your knife at 45 degrees (half a right angle) and then tilt the knife closer to the steel by half the remaining space and then by half again.

→ Then stroke the full length of the blade from top to bottom of the steel, using both sides of it. You sharpen the entire blade from the handle to the tip. MUCH safer, too.

DISHWASHER HEALTH

Knives including table knives should be put into a dishwasher with the blade down, a safety measure however they are made. This also stops water getting into the handle if the blade has a tang that is separate from the handle, which can lead to rot or the harbouring of germs.

NO PRESSURE

Do not use pressure when cutting and slicing but let a sharp knife do the work. Use light, long strokes, back and forth, using all the blade length. You'll cut through anything easily, even fresh bread, and fragile foods hold their shape.

GETTING EDGY

The sharper the knife the safer it is, because you use less pressure and do less injury if you slip. When a knife is blunt you push harder and if it slips that means any wound is deeper.

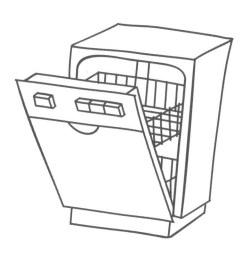

BIGGER IS BETTER

Choose a bigger, sharper knife over a small, lightweight paring or peeling knife, the favourite but awkward choice of many domestic cooks. Bigger knives give more control and their weight contributes to ease of cutting without you adding pressure.

KNIVES OUT—I

Cut fist-sized mozzarella or small bocconcini on an egg slicer. They are too rubbery for most knives and knife skills. Ditto button and small mushrooms. Saves much time.

KNIVES OUT—II

Use Nylon fishing line or non-flavoured dental floss to cut goats' cheese logs or sticky cheeses without squashing them. Slide a long length of either under the food, cross the two ends over the top, pull in opposite directions and the line or floss will cut from bottom to top.

SINK NOT

Protect ceramic sinks from cracking when cleaning heavy pots by first lining with folded wet newspaper or by laying down as many wooden spoons as you have—buy some if you don't.

19

40 FLAVOUR HACKS

Amazing affinities that put you miles ahead but take only baby steps.
Here 1+1 = 3 or more—and there are others throughout the book.

**ANGOSTURA BITTERS IN
FRUIT SALADS.**

AVOCADO AND HONEY:
works where sugar does not in
mousses, ice creams.

APPLE PIE WITH ROSE WATER:
a heritage Shaker thing to do.

BACON AND MAPLE-SYRUP:
with or without waffles.

BAY LEAF AND CREAM OR MILK:
for liquid or baked custards.

**BANANA AND CRUNCHY
PEANUT BUTTER:** but you knew
that, right?

BLACK OLIVES AND ORANGE ZEST: a little chili compound, too, or dried oregano.

BLUE CHEESE WITH VOLUPTUOUS GOLDEN DESSERT WINE: yes, not just Stilton, not only sweet red port.

BLUE CHEESE WITH RUNNY HONEY: especially with soft blue cheese and further enhanced with lime zest.

BRANDY OR RUM BUTTER WITH SWEET POTATOES: of course.

BRIE AND FRESH PEAR: unbelievable.

BRIOCHE (UNSWEETENED) WITH CAVIAR: the richness and texture work better than soggy toast; unsalted butter here, too. If you make them, add saffron.

CABBAGE WITH COARSE BLACK PEPPER: masses, when hot, drained, buttered and served pronto.

CELERY IN OXTAIL STEW: the secret.

CHOCOLATE AND PEDRO XIMENEZ (PX) SHERRY: for mousses and such.

CHRISTMAS CAKE AND CHEDDAR CHEESE—WENSLEYDALE FOR SOME.

COFFEE WITH ROAST LAMB: a Scandinavian creation.

CRYSTALLISED OR PRESERVED STEM GINGER WITH DATES AND DRIED FRUITS.

DATES AND LAMB: sliced into gravy and with a little mint.

DILL AND BLACK PEPPER: especially with garlic and a chilli to flavour Christmas vodka.

KIWI FRUIT AND PERNOD: a few drops only; extra good with prawns.

LEMON CURD AND MARMITE: honest!

LOBSTER AND BASIL: in brioche, in salads.

LYCHEES AND ROSE WATER: a fascinating sorbet.

MAPLE SYRUP ON BACON AND EGGS: it must be hot.

PASTA AND BROCCOLI: a Montalbano favourite; cook broccoli pieces for the last few minutes with the pasta, serve with olive oil and Parmesan or Grana Padano cubes.

PEANUT BUTTER AND CARAMEL: anywhere, especially muffins and brownies.

PEAR AND RASPBERRY: anyway you want it, hot, cold, iced, sweet or savoury.

PINEAPPLE AND GIN: beyond mysterious; don't add heat because gin's flavour is highly fugitive.

PINOT NOIR DRUNK WITH ROAST DUCK: counter-intuitive, but.

POTATO AND WHITE TURNIP: mash white on white with cream; called Alabaster.

PRAWNS WITH PX SHERRY: add a little to melted butter or into mayonnaise.

RASPBERRY JAM WITH CHEDDAR CHEESE: in sandwiches.

ROASTED CUMIN SEEDS ON TOMATOES: sandwiches, salads, pizza, anywhere.

RUM AND VANILLA: a background for chicken stews, foreground for muffins or icing and fillings for bigger cakes.

SMOKED SALMON AND MILD HORSERADISH: perfect sandwiches and snacks and doesn't hide the taste as lemon juice does; lots of black pepper, too.

STRAWBERRIES AND BLACK PEPPER: must be fragrant pepper and coarsely ground.

SWEDE AND CREAM SHERRY: a magical mash.

TOMATO AND ORANGE: especially as mixed juices.

WATERMELON AND FETA CHEESE: perfect salad, especially with mint or basil leaves.

INDEX